12/18

MOVIE MAGIC

SPECIAL EFFECTS

BY SARA GREEN

BLASTOFF!
DISCOVERY

BELLWETHER MEDIA • MINNEAPOLIS, MN

Blastoff! Discovery launches
a new mission: reading to learn.
Filled with facts and features, each
book offers you an exciting new
world to explore!

This edition first published in 2019 by Bellwether Media, Inc.

No part of this publication may be reproduced in whole or in
part without written permission of the publisher.
For information regarding permission, write to
Bellwether Media, Inc., Attention: Permissions Department,
6012 Blue Circle Drive, Minnetonka, MN 55343.

Library of Congress Cataloging-in-Publication Data

Names: Green, Sara, 1964- author.
Title: Special Effects / by Sara Green.
Description: Minneapolis, MN : Bellwether Media, Inc.,
    2019. | Series: Blastoff! Discovery: Movie Magic |
    Includes bibliographical references and index.
Identifiers: LCCN 2018005003 (print) | LCCN 2018016192
    (ebook) | ISBN 9781626178496 (hardcover : alk.
    paper)| ISBN 9781681035901 (ebook)
Subjects: LCSH: Cinematography–Special effects–Juvenile
    literature.
Classification: LCC TR858 (ebook) | LCC TR858 .G7355
    2019 (print) | DDC 778.5/3–dc23
LC record available at https://lccn.loc.gov/2018005003

Editor: Betsy Rathburn   Designer: Brittany McIntosh

Printed in the United States of America, North Mankato, MN.

TABLE OF CONTENTS

A PREHISTORIC MONSTER!   4

WHAT ARE SPECIAL EFFECTS?   8

INNOVATIVE IDEAS   12

BIGGER AND BETTER   20

ENDLESS POSSIBILITIES   28

GLOSSARY   30

TO LEARN MORE   31

INDEX   32

A PREHISTORIC MONSTER!

An enormous dinosaur bursts through the jungle. It has long, narrow jaws and sharp teeth. A bony fin stretches along its back. This creature is a ferocious spinosaurus! With a roar, it begins attacking people trapped in a downed plane. Will they find a way to escape?

Luckily, the dinosaur is not real. It was created using **animatronics**. The dinosaur is a special effect made for the 2001 movie *Jurassic Park III*.

JURASSIC PARK III

Designers worked hard to make the puppet look real. The dinosaur weighed 25,000 pounds (11,340 kilograms) and was nearly 45 feet (14 meters) long. Its inside was made from plastic and steel. The skin was foam rubber.

Hydraulics powered the dinosaur's movements. **Puppeteers** used remote controls to make it move. Other dinosaurs in the movie used puppeteers, too. For example, the velociraptors were controlled by a puppeteer inside the dinosaur!

ARE THEY REAL?

Some of the most famous movie characters have been animatronic. Popular examples include the shark in *Jaws* and the alien in *E.T. the Extra-Terrestrial*.

E.T.

WHAT ARE SPECIAL EFFECTS?

Special effects, also called practical effects, are tricks used by filmmakers. These effects happen on a movie **set** during a **shoot**. Filmmakers often use special effects to shoot dangerous **scenes**, such as explosions and car crashes.

Filmmakers also use special effects to make unusual things appear on screen. For example, **science fiction** movies often include special effects. They allow filmmakers to create pretend places and distant planets. Aliens and other strange creatures come to life!

THE NEVERENDING STORY II:
THE NEXT CHAPTER

WHAT'S THE DIFFERENCE?

Visual effects are another type of special effects. Visual effects may be added with a computer after the movie is already filmed.

TRANSFORMERS: REVENGE OF THE FALLEN

THE LORD OF THE RINGS:
THE FELLOWSHIP OF THE RING

MINIATURE SET

Special effects bring stories to life in many other ways. Is a storm raging on screen? On set, it is pretend. Rain falls from tall structures called rain stands. Giant fans make the wind gust!

Special effects also create new worlds. **Rigging** helps superheroes fly and leap from building to building. **Miniatures** bring fantastic worlds to life. **Director** Peter Jackson used them to create towns and cities for the Lord of the Rings film series!

HOLD ON TIGHT!

A Boeing 707 engine was used to create strong winds in some of the scenes in *Twister*, a 1996 movie about storm-chasing scientists.

INNOVATIVE IDEAS

Special effects have been used since the earliest movies. An 1895 film called *The Execution of Mary Stuart* recreated the death of a Scottish queen. Director Alfred Clark used a **substitution shot** to create the scene. It paved the way for many other movies to wow audiences with special effects.

OUCH!

Filmmaker Georges Méliès used a substitution shot in the 1902 film *A Trip to the Moon*. A famous scene shows a rocket crashing into the Moon's eye.

SPECIAL EFFECTS PIONEER

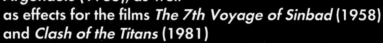

Name: Ray Harryhausen
Born: June 29, 1920, in Los Angeles, California
Famous For: Special effects artist who created the famous stop-motion skeleton fight in *Jason and the Argonauts* (1963), as well as effects for the films *The 7th Voyage of Sinbad* (1958) and *Clash of the Titans* (1981)
Awards: 1991 Gordon E. Sawyer award for technical achievement, 2011 Lifetime Achievement Award from Visual Effects Society

JASON AND THE ARGONAUTS

KING KONG

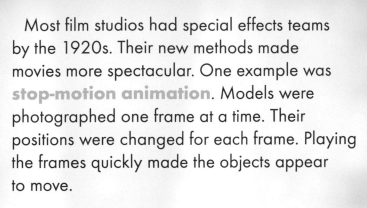

Most film studios had special effects teams by the 1920s. Their new methods made movies more spectacular. One example was **stop-motion animation**. Models were photographed one frame at a time. Their positions were changed for each frame. Playing the frames quickly made the objects appear to move.

Willis O'Brien used this method to make dinosaurs look real in the 1925 film *The Lost World*. He also brought a large ape to life in the 1933 movie *King Kong*!

PLAY WITH CLAY

Clay figures are often used in stop-motion animation because they are easy to move. This type of animation is called claymation. Holiday classics like *Rudolph the Red-Nosed Reindeer* were made with claymation.

RUDOLPH THE RED-NOSED REINDEER

Early filmmakers also found ways to create weather on screen. The 1937 film *The Hurricane* featured a huge storm. Thousands of gallons of water were poured on the set!

Movies with winter scenes also created a challenge. Filmmakers had to make fake snow. Many substances have been used, including soap flakes, sugar, and salt. *The Wizard of Oz* featured a scene where snow fell on Dorothy and her friends. The snow was really a material called **asbestos**!

THE HURRICANE

THE DAY AFTER TOMORROW

WINTER WONDERLAND

Today's filmmakers often use torn paper to make snow. The ragged pieces fall, drift, and clump like real snow.

MARY POPPINS

Filmmakers also used **matte paintings** to create landscapes and backgrounds. They filmed scenes with a painted piece of glass in between the set and the camera. This makes the painted parts of the glass look like part of the set. The added details on the glass turn ordinary objects into fantastic scenes and **props**.

An early example was in the 1964 Disney musical *Mary Poppins*. The filmmakers used many matte paintings to turn London into a magical world for Mary and her friends!

PAINTED PANES

Matte paintings were used in many scenes from the Star Wars series. Tall redwood trees were filmed through glass painted with beautiful buildings. This created the Ewok village!

BIGGER AND BETTER

Over time, filmmakers have continued to dazzle audiences with advanced special effects. Some of them use huge machines. They can create impressive scenes that appear to defy the laws of physics.

For example, the 1968 film *2001: A Space Odyssey* amazed movie audiences with its gravity-defying effects. In one scene, an astronaut jogs up the walls and across the ceiling of a spaceship. But the actor was really running in a large, rotating wheel!

2001: A SPACE ODYSSEY SET

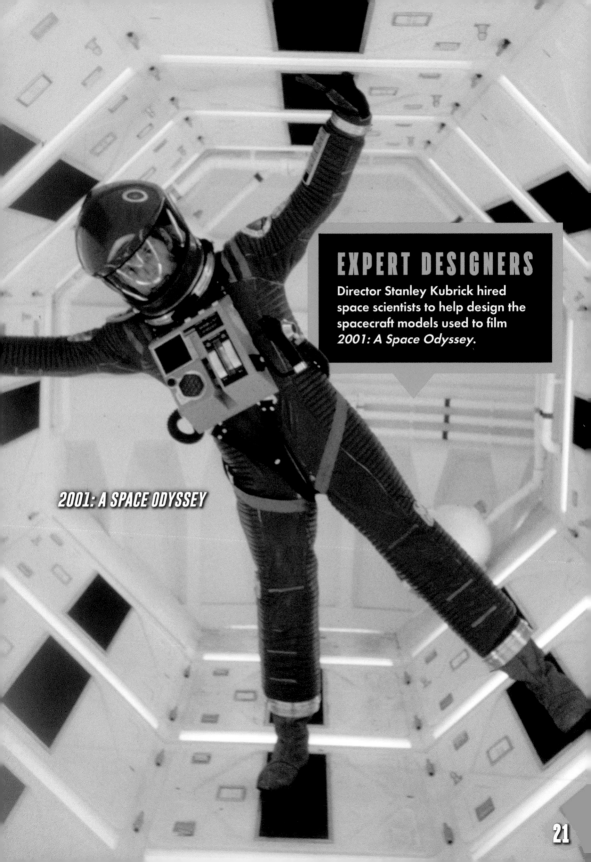

EXPERT DESIGNERS

Director Stanley Kubrick hired space scientists to help design the spacecraft models used to film *2001: A Space Odyssey*.

2001: A SPACE ODYSSEY

CONTROLLED EXPLOSION
FOR *THE AVENGERS*

Fires and explosions are common special effects used in action movies. Experts called **pyrotechnicians** make fires burn safely on movie sets. They often use fuel tanks to ignite fires. The tanks can make small flames or raging **infernos**! The fires are real but the sets do not burn down. They are made of **nonflammable** materials!

MODERN
SPECIAL EFFECTS MASTER

Name: Stan Winston
Born: April 7, 1946, in Richmond, Virginia
Famous For: Special effects artist who worked on many famous characters and creatures, including Penguin in *Batman Returns* (1992) and animatronic dinosaurs in *Jurassic Park* (1993)
Awards: 1987, 1992, and 1994 Academy Awards for Best Visual Effects

Pyrotechnicians also create safe explosions. Careful planning helps them control where pieces fly. They use special chemicals to control explosions. They also make some objects extra weak in certain spots. This makes them easier to blow up.

Blowing up small models is another way to make explosions safer. The 1996 film *Independence Day* included a scene where aliens blew up the White House. But it was really just a model!

INDEPENDENCE DAY

FAMOUS SPECIAL EFFECT

Special Effect: A model of the ship *Titanic* that was 10 stories high, 775 feet (236 meters) long, and floated in a huge tank
Movie: *Titanic*
Year: 1997
Director: James Cameron

FLYING HIGH

When characters need to fly, filmmakers often turn to rigging. These harnesses and wires help actors jump and flip with little effort. Superhero movies often use rigging to give characters superhuman powers!

*CAPTAIN AMERICA:
THE WINTER SOLDIER*

Sometimes a scene calls for bullets to hit walls. But no loaded guns are on set. How does the **crew** make the gunfire look real? A special effects expert cuts away a piece of the wall and puts in a tiny charge. It is controlled electronically.

Then, paint and fillers are used to make the wall look unmarked. At just the right moment, the expert makes the charge explode. It looks like a bullet hit the wall!

PIRATES OF THE CARIBBEAN: AT WORLD'S END

ENDLESS POSSIBILITIES

Today's filmmakers often use **CGI** to create special effects. Filmmakers add images after shooting is finished. These images are called visual effects. Storms, fires, and explosions only happen on the computer. They do not put anyone in danger!

Many settings and creatures are also created with CGI. For example, in *Star Wars: Episode II - Attack of the Clones*, Yoda was a CG character. With so many special effects available, filmmakers can make almost anything happen on screen!

PUPPET MASTER YODA

In the first three Star Wars films, Yoda was a puppet! The character returned as a puppet in 2017's *Star Wars: The Last Jedi.*

CG YODA IN
STAR WARS: EPISODE II -
ATTACK OF THE CLONES

GLOSSARY

animatronics—puppetlike machines that imitate animals

asbestos—a soft gray material; asbestos was found to be poisonous if inhaled in the twentieth century.

CGI—artwork created by computers; CGI stands for computer-generated imagery.

chemicals—substances that are used to produce a change in another substance

crew—a group of people who use special skills to help make a movie

director—a person who controls the making of a movie

hydraulics—machines powered by fluids

infernos—huge fires

matte paintings—fake sets made with paint

miniatures—small models

nonflammable—unable to burn

props—short for properties; props are the objects used by actors or set decorators in a movie.

puppeteers—people who work with puppets

pyrotechnicians—people responsible for making fires and explosions happen safely

rigging—systems of ropes, cables, wires, and other types of support used by actors

scenes—parts of a film

science fiction—pretend stories based on future science; science fiction movies often feature space and life on other planets.

set—the place where a movie or film is made

shoot—the act of filming a movie

stop-motion animation—a technique where objects are moved a tiny bit between frames; when the frames are played back, the objects appear to move on their own.

substitution shot—a type of shot in which a camera is stopped and the actors freeze while an object or actor is exchanged for another

TO LEARN MORE

AT THE LIBRARY

Bradley, Timothy J. *History of Monster Movies.*
Huntington Beach, Calif.: Teacher Created
Materials, 2017.

Miles, Liz. *Movie Special Effects.* Chicago, Ill.:
Raintree, 2010.

Mullins, Matt. *Special Effects Technician.* Ann Arbor,
Mich.: Cherry Lake Publishing, 2012.

ON THE WEB

Learning more about
special effects is as easy
as 1, 2, 3.

1. Go to www.factsurfer.com.

2. Enter "special effects" into the search box.

3. Click the "Surf" button and you will see a list of
   related web sites.

With factsurfer.com, finding more information is just
a click away.

INDEX

2001: A Space Odyssey, 20, 21

animatronics, 4, 7

bullets, 27

car crashes, 8

CGI, 28, 29

Clark, Alfred, 12

claymation, 15

Execution of Mary Stuart, The, 12

explosions, 8, 22, 23, 24, 27, 28

Harryhausen, Ray, 13

Hurricane, The, 16

hydraulics, 7

Independence Day, 24

Jackson, Peter, 11

Jurassic Park III, 4, 5, 7

King Kong, 14, 15

Kubrick, Stanley, 21

Lord of the Rings, The (series), 10, 11

Lost World, The, 15

Mary Poppins, 18, 19

matte paintings, 19

Méliès, Georges, 12

miniatures, 10, 11

models, 21, 24, 25

O'Brien, Willis, 15

puppets, 7, 28

pyrotechnicians, 23, 24

rain stands, 11

rigging, 11, 26

science fiction, 8

Star Wars (series), 19, 28, 29

stop-motion animation, 15

substitution shot, 12

Titanic, 25

Trip to the Moon, A, 12

Twister, 11

visual effects, 9, 28

weather, 11, 16, 17, 28

Winston, Stan, 23

Wizard of Oz, The, 16

The images in this book are reproduced through the courtesy of: Jonathan Hordle/ AP Images, front cover, p. 3; AF Archive/ Alamy, pp. 4, 4-5, 6-7, 7, 8, 11, 12, 13 (top, bottom), 16, 23, 27; Paramount/ Everett Collection, pp. 8-9; New Line Cinema/ Photofest Digital, pp. 10 (top), 10-11; World History Archive/ Alamy, p. 13 (bottom); Everett Collection, pp. 14-15; Paul Fearn/ Alamy, p. 15; 20th Century Fox Film Corp./ Everett Collection, pp. 16-17, 24, 24-25; Entertainment Pictures/ Alamy, pp. 18-19; Twentieth Century Fox Film Corp./ Photofest Digital, p. 19; Dmitri Kessel/ Getty Images, p. 20; The LIFE Picture Collection/ Getty Images, p. 21; Splash News/ Alamy, pp. 22-23; Pictorial Press Ltd/ Alamy, p. 24; Walt Disney Studios Motion Pictures/ Everett Collection, pp. 26-27; Dylan Martinez/ Newscom, p. 28; Lucasfilm Ltd/ Photofest Digital, p. 29.